C0-AVG-422

Mark Riddle

THE (UN)OFFICIAL CHURCH STAFF MANUAL

YOUTH PASTOR EDITION

ZONDERVAN®

ZONDERVAN.com/
AUTHORTRACKER
follow your favorite authors

youth specialties

YOUTH SPECIALTIES

The (un) Official Church Staff Manual
Copyright 2009 by Mark Riddle

Youth Specialties resources, 1890 Cordell Ct. Ste. 105, El Cajon, CA 92020 are published by Zondervan, 5300 Patterson Ave. SE, Grand Rapids, MI 49530.

ISBN 978-0-310-28366-9

All Scripture quotations, unless otherwise indicated, are taken from the *Holy Bible, Today's New International Version*™. TNIV®. Copyright 2001, 2005 by International Bible Society. Used by permission of Zondervan. All rights reserved.

Any Internet addresses (websites, blogs, etc.) and telephone numbers printed in this book are offered as a resource. They are not intended in any way to be or imply an endorsement by Youth Specialties, nor does Youth Specialties vouch for the content of these sites and numbers for the life of this book.

Cover & Interior design by SharpSeven Design
Illustrations by Barak Hardley

Printed in the United States of America

09 10 11 12 13 14 • 20 19 18 17 16 15 14 13 12 11 10 9 8 7 6 5 4 3 2 1

CONTENTS

SPECIAL ACKNOWLEDGMENTS

Thanks to Pam, Zach, Jaden, and Mikayla.

Thanks to the people of Capital Hill, St. Mark's, Asbury, Kirk of the Hills, Bella Vista, Something, and Eikon. Much of what I write about in this book was made evident to me through you.

Thanks to my former senior pastors: Paul, Darrell, Tom, and John F. God has used you to help shape who I am today. I'm grateful for your leadership.

Thanks to my man John Raymond.

Thanks to David Welch, Jay Howver, and the rest of the YS/Zondervan team.

A special shout out to all the people who complained about me as a youth pastor and the handful of people who, over the years, felt it was their job to drive me from leadership. I really have learned a lot from you as well. I'm a better, more compassionate, and hopefully more Christ-like person because of it.

Thanks to those of you who gave me feedback on this book: Len, Bob, Todd, G-Man, Dan, and Dino.

Thanks to Jonathan, Todd, Jason J., Damien, Scott, and Kerry for being on the Riddle Group team. Your collective wisdom is staggering to me.

I'm grateful for the opportunity to learn from the churches The Riddle Group has partnered with. It's a privilege to work with and learn from you.

Thanks to my friends who gave me feedback along the way.

DEDICATION

For Zachery, Jaden, and Mikayla. You help me see the world in ways I never dreamed I could. Thanks for your joy, laughter, and love for life. Each of you is unique, and you make me laugh in unique ways. Words fall short in describing how deeply I love each of you. Being your dad, I have the honor of seeing you learn about the story of God and the world we live in. You bring me tremendous joy.

INTRODUCTION

It's a rough world out there, and you often have to learn along the way—usually by trial and error. There are some mistakes you make only once. Having middle school boys put their shoes into a stinking pile for a quick crowd breaker in a small, not-so-ventilated youth room will never happen again on your watch. You can now advise your peers who insist on playing the game that it's a good idea to have a stash of barf bags on hand for the girls. You can offer that advice because you didn't have barf bags on hand, and the smell from that night is burned so deeply into your memory that you can taste it right now.

What other job requires a person to be able to do so many things that are meaningful for ministry but completely irrelevant outside the church? Yes, it's a rough world out there. And there's a lot at stake. Being a youth pastor requires the unique ability to present the serious and the silly—often within moments of each other. It's a job that requires discernment.

This book may help in that area. It too presents the serious and the silly. I'll leave it to you (and your discernment) to tell which is which—and to identify the point of each list. In each chapter, you'll find lessons I've learned over the years—though they may not always be obvious. I'd say this book is intended to help you avoid some of the mistakes I've made, but that would only be partially true. The fact is, following some of the instructions in this book will cause you to fail—and then help you grow as a result.

Good luck!

Mark Riddle
Tulsa, Oklahoma
Markriddle.net

9

Section 1:

WORKING WITH INTERESTING PEOPLE

How to Brown-Nose Your Senior Pastor

Every youth pastor knows that in order to survive the demands of leading a youth ministry, you must stay on the good side of the senior pastor. A good relationship with your senior pastor can go a long way toward fulfilling your plans for ministry.

Here are nine ways to develop a good relationship the old-fashioned way: By brown-nosing your boss.

1. Compliment him on his tie (or her brooch). Do so at least once a week.

2. On Sunday mornings place yourself in the front row. Sit on the edge of your seat with a look on your face that says, "These are the most amazing words that have ever been spoken." Take notes. Afterward, tell your pastor that her delivery was flawless, saying, "God spoke to me during your second point." For extra emphasis, add the phrase "...in a powerful way!"

3. Every senior pastor is known for liking something specific, whether it's bow ties, college sports, Precious Moments collectibles, movies, or something else. Procure these items and distribute them at regular intervals and on special occasions.

4. Be a responsible adult. (Google it.)

5. Attend a conference with your senior pastor. When the speaker says something brilliant, lean over and say, "That comment reminds me of something you've said before!"

6. Show up ~~early~~ ... ~~on time~~ ... no more than five minutes late to staff meetings.

7. Get your senior pastor ~~an iTunes giftcard~~ a Lawrence Welk album.

8. Remember this phrase: "Your eschatological constructs continually remind me of Moltmann's theology of hope—and it's inspiring me to live like Jesus!"

9. Play the pastor in one-on-one basketball in the church gym. Let the pastor win.

How to Cope While Running the Soundboard

Because you're a team player and the only person on staff aside from the music minister who's technologically competent enough to run the soundboard, occasionally you may find yourself in the back of the sanctuary with a pair of headphones over your ears.

If you find yourself in such a position, don't panic. Here's what you need to remember.

SETUP

1. Turn the power on. The switch is generally a combo of power strips, amplifiers, and power buttons. Plan on spending five minutes trying to figure out just the right combination that actually turns everything on.

2. Pick up the headphones.

3. Check the headphones for lice.

4. Admit to yourself your appearance concerns. Unlike the guy who regularly runs the soundboard, you don't think you look cool wearing these beasts.

5. Put them on anyway. It's for Jesus.

6. Play with the phantom power button.

WORKING THE BOARD

1. When running a sound check, it's good to keep in mind that the following things are completely normal:

    a. The woman who can't sing and plays the tambourine will want to hear more of her voice in the monitors.

    b. The bass player will turn down the volume on his instrument for you during sound check but turn it back up during the worship service.

    c. Someone—very likely an associate pastor—will come over to give you advice. He claims he doesn't know anything about sound, which is why he lets you run the board. But at this moment he sees himself as an expert. He might say something like, "The blend isn't very good."

    d. The worship leader, who's an artist and doesn't deal well with confrontations, will privately instruct you to turn someone in the band way down—or off—during the worship service because the person sounds bad. That way the worship leader doesn't ever have to tell the person to leave the worship team.

2. When running sound during a worship service, it's good to keep in mind that the following things are completely normal:

    a. The guitarist will plug herself in while the line is hot, and it will make a loud pop.

    b. Someone old will tell you that the volume is too loud.

    c. Someone will give you unsolicited advice on the mix.

d. The pastor will pick up the mic, walk directly in front of a speaker, and then give you a dirty look when the feedback starts.

e. A member of the program team will give you a homemade video that was recorded too loudly. The volume will create distortion in the playback, which you cannot fix.

f. You will receive more dirty looks.

g. You will have to resist the urge to take all of the bass and mid-range from the preacher's mic.

3. When faced with individuals who are critical of your sound mixing, it's important to remember one of these two phrases, which have been passed on by professional sound engineers.

a. "Garbage in, garbage out."

b. "It's hard to polish a turd."

Adjustable band.

Big foam cushions that make your ears sweat.

Unknown grimy DNA material left from the real sound person.

Check for lice.

Spiral cord that's always tangled.

How Not to Start a Sermon in Church

Occasionally the senior pastor will you let you preach in the big church service. When that happens, you'll want to make the most of the opportunity. In order to do that, you'll need to get your sermon off on the right foot with a memorable quote or anecdote. You'll need to choose wisely, though. Not all memorable sermon starters will have the desired effect. Here are few you may want to avoid.

- "There once was a man from Nantucket ..."

- "We've locked all the doors. There's no way out."

- "Bring out the snakes!"

- "I had a dream of a 900-foot Jesus."

- "Some of you may have realized that I'm not wearing any pants."

- "I know secrets about all you people, so listen carefully or I'll lob a few personal examples in my sermon this morning."

- "Today I will mime the entire service."

- "To the person who wrote me that anonymous note last Monday: Kiss my butt!"

- "To the person who wrote me that anonymous note last Wednesday: The feeling's mutual. Call me sometime."

- "Shooodahboaguhtahonda!"

- "Some of you know my story. You know that I lived a wild life before I met the Lord. But I'll bet none of you knew that I used to be a woman."

- "During our 32-week study of Isaiah, I will preach as Isaiah did. For some of you it might be uncomfortable to see your youth pastor preaching naked. But please understand that it's biblical. At the end of our study, we'll do a short study on Hosea, then finish up the year with a stimulating series on Onan."

- "You'll have to excuse me. I was out all night trying to witness to the folks at the corner bar, and I've got a killer hangover."

- "Everyone hold up your Bibles and repeat after me, 'This is my Bible. I am who it says I am....'"

How to Survive the Post-Youth Event Attack

It's inevitable. After you spend a weekend overseeing a wildly successful youth retreat, you'll come home to find IT waiting for you. The dreaded email message. Someone is hunting youth workers again, and you're right in the crosshairs.

Your joy over the decisions your kids have made will quickly fade as you try to process the anger and disappointment directed at you. Unless, of course, you know the secret to surviving such an attack.

BEFORE THE RETREAT

1. Go to your desk.

2. Get a piece of fluorescent yellow paper, a roll of duct tape, and a red Magnum permanent marker from your desk.

3. Write "DUCK!" on the fluorescent paper and use the duct tape to attach it to your door at eye level.

AFTER THE RETREAT

1. Enter the church.

2. Read your sign as you enter your office.

3. Remember that it's normal for a post-event attack to occur. Expecting an attack will help you adjust your attitude, so that your response won't be too dramatic.

THE RESPONSE

If necessary, use the following form to respond to the email message. [I've included my comments in brackets.]

Dear (insert name of complainer),

I just received your email this morning when I got into the office. First, I must say that I appreciate your colorful use of the English language. I am delighted by your frequent use of the phrase "them kids." And I was riveted by your description of the youth group as "showen no respect buy trashin the churches van." [Such niceties set a convivial tone for the letter. Who doesn't appreciate a compliment? If the writer's literary achievements are duly noted, he may be more likely to continue reading your reply.]

I also appreciate that you chose not to gossip and came directly to me with your issue, thus living out the principles of Matthew 18. [Okay, look, this is a church. No one ever goes directly to the person he has an issue with. I've found the preceding passive-aggressive language is helpful both in making the complainer feel guilty and share the blame for bad behavior. Of course, such a reply is completely unbiblical. But this is church. If you're going to work here, you're going to need some chops.]

Of course, I want to meet personally with you ASAP so that we can discuss this urgent and important matter and resolve it quickly.

In Christ,

(insert your name)

How to Keep Church People from Bothering You During Your Staycation

Not every vacation involves traveling. Staying home for vacation is known as a "staycation." (On a vacation, you leave. On a staycation, you stay.) The problem with a staycation is that if church people know you're around, they'll try to contact you when needs arise. Obviously you can't lie to them about your vacation plans. But you can play an intricate word game with them. All you need are a couple of playful and willing accomplices. Here's what you do.

1. During the weeks leading up to your time off, don't tell anyone where you're going. Instruct your spouse and children to do the same.

2. When students, youth workers, and staff members ask where you'll be going on your vacation, say, "It's a secret," in a joking tone of voice. Then change the subject.

3. Continue not to tell anyone where you're going.

4. Pick a faraway place that doesn't sound glamorous: Saskatoon, Saskatchewan, Santa Fe, Edina, or any city in Texas. You're not going there, but you need to decide on a name.

5. Choose two accomplices: Your most trusted youth volunteer and a trusted office staff person. Involve no one else.

6. Here comes the word game. Say this exact sentence to each accomplice: "Something about Saskatoon (or whatever place you choose)."

7. While you're gone, if someone approaches these individuals to inquire where you went, they can respond in total truthfulness, "He said something about Saskatoon."

8. Mission accomplished.

How to Make a Creepy Bible Halloween Costume for the "Church Carnival"

If your church holds a "carnival" on Halloween, you may be expected to wear a Bible character costume. It's a totally lame idea, but it's one that's often used. If that's your situation, I feel your pain. I also know from experience that dressing up as Lucifer, demons, or Jesus on the cross generally doesn't lend itself to a festive environment.

Because you canceled youth group for Halloween and convinced some middle school kids to work the carnival, you're under the gun to find something cool and out-of-the-ordinary to wear. You need to find a biblical costume a youth pastor would wear. Look no further.

WHAT YOU'LL NEED
- A broom handle
- A long-haired wig
- A bottle of ketchup
- A 3- to 5-foot-long tree branch
- A white bed sheet

Step 1
Drape the bed sheet around you like a robe. It's very important that the sheet be white.

Step 2
Put on the long-haired wig. Use glue, if necessary.

Step 3

Tangle the tree branch into the wig, so that it stays firmly rooted in the hair.

Step 4

Pour the bottle of ketchup all over your stomach and back. Add a touch to your mouth and eyes for dramatic effect.

Step 5

Carefully break the broom handle in half. Chances are, it will look like a spear. Put one half of the handle in front of yourself, the other half in back.

Voila! You are Absalom, son of King David, just after he was killed by Joab.

How to Survive a Surprise Parents' Meeting

Nobody likes a surprise—unless it's a party celebrating how great you are. Meetings in which parents secretly organize themselves to talk about their frustrations with the youth pastor and the youth ministry are a painful reality in too many churches. Such meetings feel like betrayal and can leave you questioning yourself and your calling.

More and more senior pastors understand how damaging these meetings can be to the church and the youth ministry. Unfortunately, not all senior pastors have the power or authority to stop them from happening.

If you ever have to face an ad hoc parents' meeting, here are a few tips to keep in mind.

1. When you walk into the room, you'll be surprised and very uncomfortable. Many people will be watching you. Others won't look you in the eye. Take a deep breath. How you handle this meeting is very important. Parents hold these meetings for two reasons. First, to get rid of their youth pastor. Second, to open a conversation about issues they feel need to be addressed. You won't be able to determine which kind of meeting this is. Chances are it's both.

   On the other hand, statistically speaking, you won't be at that church in a couple of years anyway. After you're gone you'll probably have trouble remembering any of the names of the people you're getting ready to meet with. So don't sweat it.

2. Listen. There's something for you to learn in this situation. What is it? As wrong as this kind of meeting feels (and, make no question about it, it is very

wrong), take the road of humility and listen. It's a sure bet some people in the room feel as though they haven't been heard. Listen to them. What are they trying to communicate? What are the underlying assumptions they hold that led them to these questions?

3. If you're given a chance to speak…
  • Reflect on what you hear people say.

  • Ask questions.

  • Answer questions and bring clarity. But keep in mind that many people simply want to be heard and may not be looking for answers.

  • Offer sincere apologies when they're called for. (My experience is that there is always something I can apologize for. Have the integrity to say, "I'm sorry.")

  • Don't be reactionary. Avoid comments like these:
    a. "Ever read Matthew 18, you unbiblical jerks?!"
    b. "I'm wondering if I should just call you all Judas from now on."
    c. "Some of you are smarter than this."
    d. "I'd expect this from a few of you, but the rest of you have gone above and beyond my expectations for being lemmings."
    e. "Who do you think you are? Peons are what you are! Nothing! If I wanted to know what you thought, I'd ask you!"

- *Don't* avoid pointed questions.
  a. "Jill, when we spoke last week, I asked you if you had any issues with me or the student ministry. And you said, 'No.' How could you say that and still lead this meeting now?"
  b. "Bob, we've talked about this before, and you told me we'd solved the problem."
  c. "Is this the first time you've met?"
  d. "How did this meeting come about?"

- Tell them briefly (in a sentence or two) how this kind of meeting makes you feel.

4. Leave the meeting and call your senior pastor.

5. Be prepared to be disappointed in a few people. As a leader in the congregation, you need to recognize that people don't always behave in the best possible way. Occasionally you'll feel the brunt of this behavior. Don't let bad behavior come as a total surprise.

6. Remind yourself that you're in good company. Jesus had meetings like these.

How to Keep Your Cool When You Receive an Anonymous Email

Every youth pastor receives anonymous criticism. You can spot such a message almost immediately, even when the author tries to offer an awkward compliment before launching into the criticism.

Here's an easy, nine-step process for responding to anonymous potshots in a healthy way.

Step 1

If it's an email message, print it. Then delete it from your inbox. DO NOT ATTEMPT TO READ IT. Go to the church kitchen and get a stainless steel mixing bowl.

Step 2

Extend your arms forward, holding the paper with two hands approximately one inch apart from each other at the top of the page.

THE ECO-FRIENDLY RESPONSE

Step 1
Don't print the email.

Step 2
Hit delete and say goodbye to the anonymous letter.

Step 3

Holding the paper firmly with your fingertips, make a quick motion with your right hand toward your body with enough force to tear the paper completely in half.

Step 4

You will now have two pieces of paper. Place one on top of the other and repeat Steps 2 and 3.

Step 5

Repeat Step 4 until you're left with several very small pieces of paper.

Step 6

Place the mixing bowl on the floor and the paper in mixing bowl.

Step 7

Take a lighter from your desk drawer and light the paper fragments.

Step 8

Dance[1] around mixing bowl on the floor, waving your arms in the air. Singing adds a nice touch—but is not necessary.

Step 9

Read the note. If it's not legible, discard it in a safe place and simply remember your positive experience with this paper.

THE UNHEALTHY RESPONSE

Step 1

Read the whole email.

Step 2

Get emotional about it and scream long and loud.

Step 3

CC: the email to all your staff.

Step 4

Write a bulk mail response to the entire congregation with the heading, "To the idiot who wrote me the anonymous email."

Step 5

Mention it during Sunday morning services saying, "Whoever sent me that anonymous email, you are a loser and a coward, and I have a hunch Jesus is mad at you."

Step 6

Keep the email.

---

[1] If you're a Baptist who doesn't dance, stand with your arms crossed and think about dancing. Or simply "function" around the bowl. Morning calisthenics or aerobics could also be done in place of dancing.

How to Get Fired

Important: This is not a comprehensive list.

1. Try to cast the devil out of your senior pastor.

2. Blog publicly about your ministry using your real name and real situations.

3. Use the word *crap* in front of middle school students.

4. Get caught with this book in your office.

5. Forget to put the retreat pictures on the youth bulletin board.

6. Use phrases like, "If you really loved Jesus, then you'd do what I'm telling you to do" or "God told me to tell you to do what I say."

7. Provide one-to-one counseling sessions for someone of the opposite sex.

8. After youth group, drive kids of the opposite sex home alone.

9. Ignore the advice people in your church give you.

10. Talk poorly about your senior pastor.

11. Don't try to understand why things are the way they are in your church.

Section 2:
DOING
YOUTH WORK

How to Name Your Youth Ministry

There are few things as important as having a memorable youth ministry name. Veteran youth pastors know that it's not about the content of the ministry, but rather how hip, cool, and catchy the ministry's moniker is. Branding is the new evangelism.

You want a name that represents who you are and what your ministry is about. A few youth pastors who've been to seminary might propose a Greek word, but the rest of us know there's a good reason New Testament Greek is no longer spoken.

Your name must also represent Christ, his Kingdom, and the amazing love of God. With that in mind, there are a few main themes in the youth ministry culture you should be aware of.

1. Youth groups named after natural disasters—Tsunami, Aftershock, Quake, Wildfire—are popular choices. Nothing communicates the love of God like the destruction of entire islands and cities and the death of thousands of people.

2. Youth ministries named for military terms—Ground Zero, Crossfire, Basic Training—have become culturally relevant since 9/11. Nothing says, "We love you" to unchurched kids like declaring war on them.

3. Naming your youth ministry after mental trauma or illness can really get your kids pumped up. Mania is a favorite of many churches. Since *mania* is mental illness marked by periods of great excitement and delusions, it makes a great fit for your church. Other names you might consider, for obvious reasons, are Asylum, Rage, and Crazy.

4. Similar to names for mental trauma are names for violent acts or pain. Ministries named Epidemic, Blind

Sided, and Third Degree Burn all reflect unpleasant experiences you normally wouldn't want to be associated with. But that stigma can be overcome. Even better are youth groups with death-related names such as D.O.A., Code Blue, and the ever-enjoyable Flatline. These groups sound like places where you need to die to yourself, but make sure you have a signed medical release from all the kids attending.

5. Use of the word "Fire" is common for youth groups because they want their kids to be "on fire." This comes from Jesus' mandate to "acquire the fire" and be "on-fire Christians."[2]

6. Scientific terms are also increasingly popular. Names like Velocity, H2O, Catalyst, Apex, and Momentum are being used by growing, theologically conservative ministries. The use of such scientific terms seems to point to the evangelical church's growing readiness to embrace modern scientific thought.

7. Acronyms are very popular, too. R.I.O.T., A.L.I.E.N., A.T.T.A.C.K., H.A.N.G.A.R., B.A.R.F., and D.U.N.G. are just a few of the acronym names that have been snatched up by youth ministries around the country.

Beware: It's easy to get carried away with acronyms. There are youth group names that appear to be nothing but a random gathering of letters and numbers. Names like 311, 4gvn, UMYF, and 1229 all mean something to you, but not to anyone outside your walls. Random letters and numbers are best used when you don't really want anyone outside your little group to know anything about who you are and what you do. The use of obscure numbers and letters

---

[2] Okay, Jesus never actually said that (and neither did any other biblical writer). But we all believe he did, so get over it.

is a sure way to communicate to people outside your ministry that they're not welcome.

8. If you struggle to find a name that best represents your church, a good fallback strategy is to employ the letter "X" in the name. Xtreme, BRIX, eXcite, eXcellence, GenX, neXgen, and X factor are all good "Xamples" of "X" names. "X" will never go out of style, because it's biblical.

For a more complete look at youth group naming possibilities, consult the following table, which has been arranged by category.

NATURAL DISASTERS	ACRONYMS
After Shock	A.L.I.E.N.
Earthquake	A.L.I.V.E.
Epicenter	A.T.T.A.C.K.
Eye of the Storm	B.A.R.F.
The Flood	D.U.N.G.
Storm Surge	H.A.N.G.A.R.
Tidal Wave	R.I.O.T.
Tsunami	
Wildfire	

MILITARY

Armed for Battle

Armored Youth

Army

AWOL

Ballistic Youth

The Barracks

Basic Training

Battle Cry

Blast

B.O.M.B.

BUNKER

CIA

Code Red

COPS

Crossfire

Crusaders (Nothing says the love of Jesus like a reference to a historical campaign of death, torture, and coercion.)

Da Bomb

Devil Stompin' Army

Drop Zone

FBI

FORCE

Ground Zero

Heir Force

Hissoldiers

Invasion

J.R.O.T.C.

New Life Warriors

Pointman

RAID

Revolution

S.W.A.T.

TNT

The Underground

W.A.R.

Weapon Youth

FOOD

Bread

Common Cup

Common Grounds

C.O.R.N.B.R.E.A.D.

Crave

SALSA

SALT

MENTAL DURESS

ASYLUM

CRAZY

MAD

Mania

RAGE

Shock

SCIENCE

Accelerator (This one has science and fire.)

Afterglow

Altered

Anti Gravity

APEX

AXIS

CATALYST

Conbustion (spelled wrong)

ECHO

Element 78

Flashpoint

Fusion

H2O

Momentum

Nucleus

Nytro

180

Ozone

Radius

Velocity

Vortex

FIRE
Acquire the Fire

BLAZE

ENFUEGO

FIRE

Fire Escape

Firehouse

Fireproof

FireStorm

FLAMERZ

Ignite

Inferno

Inner Fire

P.Y.R.O.M.A.N.I.A.C.S.

PAIN AND SICKNESS
Blind Sided

Burn Unit

Cage

Chaos

CRASH

Epidemic

E.R.

Impact

The Third Degree [Burn]

CLASSIC '80S MOVIES
Alien Nation

Breakfast Club

DEATH
Code Blue

D.O.A.

Flatline

OBSCURE NUMBERS AND LETTERS

A2J

HSHO (High School Hang Out)

N10SFYD (Intensified)

UMYF

1229

24/7

3:11

4gvn

4:12

UNCLASSIFIABLE

Gospelitus

POOP (People All Over People...somehow the explanation doesn't help)

Q-Tip (Digging Deeper into God's Word)

THUGS (Teenage Homies Using God)

X

BRIX

eXcellence

eXcite

GenX

neXgen

X factors

Xtreme

How to Carry on a Conversation When You Don't Know Someone's Name

There are simply too many names to remember in youth ministry. And you have more important things to do with your time—like work on your sermon or shop for a five-gallon vat of chocolate pudding. Until you get around to learning the names of the students God has called you to pour your leftover time into, it's a good idea to fake it. Here's how.

When you meet a kid whose name you don't know, it's best to keep a few things in mind:

1. Once a kid tells you her name, she expects you to know it forever. The exception to this rule is the kid who never actually told you her name, but still expects you to know it.

2. Sometimes clothing will give you a clue. Cheerleaders and athletes often have their names stitched on their jackets.

3. If you teach the other youth workers to use kids' names when they're around you, you'll make it easier to file away some of those names in your short-term memory.

4. There will be times when you know a kid—maybe even very well—but still forget his name.

5. If you're smooth about it, you can insert one of the following generic terms in place of the student's name.
    • "My man" ("What's up, *my man!*")
    • "Bro" ("How was school today, *bro?*")
    • "Sister" ("Hey, *sister,* have I told you how cool you are recently?")

- "My friend" ("How are you doing since your parent's divorce, *my friend*?")
- "Kiddo" ("Hey, *kiddo*, where are you going?")
- "Girl" ("How have you been, *girl*?")

There are, of course, some notable exceptions to this rule. The following terms are generally viewed as unacceptable and should be avoided at all costs:

- "Ugly" ("What's up, *ugly*!")
- "Dork" ("Hey, *dork*, where'd you get those shoes?")
- "Girl" (when talking to a guy) ("You go, *girl*!")
- "Shortie" ("Hi, *shortie*! How's the weather down there?")

6. If possible, try to steer the conversation toward one of the kid's friends—someone whose name you know. Using the friend's name will reinforce to the student that you are competent enough to remember names.

7. Pray the kids don't quiz you on their names. More than likely, this will happen to you at some point—maybe even two or three years into your ministry. You'll be leading a group of students whose names you absolutely should know. One of the kids will pick up on the fact that you never directly address any of them. And then the questions will come. "Do you even know our names?" "What are they?"

8. At some point, it's best to come clean about your nomenclatural amnesia. Though the kids may not completely understand, they'll certainly get the message. Here are a couple of approaches you might try.

- "You teens all look the same to me."
- "There are so many of you. How could I possibly take the time to learn your names? You're like ants running all over the place around here."

- "Look, I have no excuse. I blew it. There are kids in the group whose names I don't know. But I know all of you."

How to Talk an Eighth-Grade Girl Down from a Sugar High

In order to properly talk an eighth-grade girl down from a sugar high, you must first identify the signs of "sugar highness." While many of these signs are often normally present in a middle school girl, a female early adolescent with a sugar high will likely exhibit ALL of them.

SIGNS OF AN EIGHTH-GRADE GIRL ON A SUGAR HIGH

1. She wears a big smile.

2. When she's not smiling, she's talking.

3. One word: *Bouncing.*

4. Her eyes are glazed over (like a Krispy Kreme doughnut).

5. She has a burning desire to tell you how she got high, which usually involves one of the following methods:
   - Excessive beverage consumption ("I drank, like, eight Mountain Dews!")
   - Inappropriate use of condiments ("I ate, like, six sugar packets at dinner!")
   - Candy ("I just love candy!")

6. She'll have a friend who's high, too. (Kids rarely get high on sugar by themselves.)

7. She'll ask you a lot of questions so you'll notice her.

8. Her friends will be giggling, in closely formed clusters on the floor, all night long.

HOW TO TALK AN EIGHTH-GRADE GIRL DOWN FROM A SUGAR HIGH

You can't.

Games You'll Play Only Once with Your Youth Group

1. Sardines
   Kids hide open cans of sardines around the church and then try to find them all.

2. Leech Fishing
   In that particularly nasty part of the river at church camp, have two kids wade into the water for five minutes. The one who emerges with the most leeches wins!

3. Telephone Relay Race (Vomit Style)
   A "fresh" take on an old game. Instead of passing a sentence from one person's ear to the next, have contestants puke on the next person. See which team can get to the end of the line first.

4. Fly Swatter Tag
   Give each kid a fly swatter and play tag. Everyone's "It."

5. Dirty Diaper Softball

6. Christian and the Lions

7. Is This Coffee Hot?

8. Ultimate Darts
   A variation of ultimate Frisbee

9. Paint the Freshman

10. Sword Drills
    With real swords.

11. Minor Surgery

How to Survive a Teen Prank

Two of the best things about working with adolescents are their mischievousness and their inclination toward fun. That combination often leads to pranks. Whether it's a spontaneous act of tossing the youth pastor into the pool or a premeditated water-balloon assault from the church roof, you *will* eventually find yourself the victim of a prank.

With that writing on the wall, there are a couple things you need to know. First, teen pranks are generally not a sign of maliciousness or intent to harm. In fact, they're often a sign of love and affection. Second, teens can read your receptivity to pranks exceptionally well—and they'll generally choose a prank that stretches your limits.

For example, let's say toilet-papering your office is a Level-1 prank, ambushing you with shaving cream is a Level-5 prank, and duct-taping you to a tree in your swimsuit and writing on your face with a Sharpie is a Level-10 prank. If, on that scale, you see yourself as having a Level-4 tolerance for pranks, you can expect a shaving cream assault (or a Level-5 equivalent) sometime in the near future.

In time, you'll develop an almost mystical sense of impending pranks—something akin to Spiderman's "Spidey-sense" or a Jedi's use of "the Force." It's a sense sharpened by experience. The more you find yourself on the business end of an over-inflated water balloon or a toothpaste tube filled with Preparation H, the better equipped you are to sniff out a prank before it's pulled. I call this supernatural awareness "prankin-sense." If you're just getting your feet wet as a youth worker, rest assured that you have no prankin-sense whatsoever. That feeling you're feeling is paranoia, which is very different from prankin-sense, but often equally beneficial.

Over the years, many youth pastors have refined the ability to see water balloons falling from rooftops, smell shaving cream through a closed cabin door, and know when a gang of high school guys is waiting to throw you into a swimming pool.

If you're a young youth pastor, you may be able to dodge eggs like Neo dodges bullets in *The Matrix*. But it's only a matter of time before you're overwhelmed by the cunning and raw number of teens hunting you down, eager to leave you lying in the fetal position on the ground in the corner of some sophomore's backyard, with a messy combo of silly string, egg, and Gillette foam on your new Abercrombie carpenter pants and weathered American Eagle rugby shirt.

WORDS OF WISDOM

1. Beware! Teen pranks can happen any time.

2. Keep a spare set of clothing with you at all times.

3. Never let a high school student with a driver's license borrow your car keys. Ever. If you need something from your car, ask a middle school girl you trust to retrieve it. (High school guys can hear car keys rattle from up to a mile away, so take precautions.) Also, never leave your keys lying around the high school youth room.

4. Before you arrive for Bible study at a house with a pool, remove all valuables from your pockets, including cell phones, wallets, watches, and loose-fitting jewelry.

5. Beware of plastic wrap at all times—especially in the bathroom or while sleeping in a bunk bed.

6. Keep a few car-wash tokens in your glove compartment at all times. You never know when you might need them.

7. Never—under any circumstances—purchase, rent, or lease a house with trees in the yard. Trees are the enemy of youth pastors.

8. If you ever decide to prank someone yourself, keep in mind that teen pranks escalate at a disturbing rate. The Lord says vengeance is *his*. You might want to repeat that to yourself a few times before you pull a prank that provokes a nuclear response (powered by youthful exuberance). At minimum, the escalation will likely end with an injury and a visit with at least one parent. It's often better just to take the first prank and turn the other cheek. [Note: You will not follow this advice.]

FOUR ROLES KIDS PLAY IN A PRANK

1. Inventor

This is the kid who came up with the idea—the little demon spawn whose imagination for destruction comes at your expense.

2. Inventor's Friends

These are the kids who, upon hearing the idea, encourage the Inventor to take action. They'll likely help gather the materials and join the inventor in executing the prank. [Note: At least one of them won't be able to throw water balloons any higher than your belt.]

3. The Mover

This is the kid who moves you into the ambush. The Mover did not invent the prank. The Mover was likely recruited at the last moment so that the Inventor and the Inventor's Friends could execute the prank.

4. Onlooker

This person finds out about the prank moments before you do. The more Onlookers who are present, the more glory there is for the Inventor—and the more embarrassment there is for you.

9. Be cautious of teens who say, "I want to show you something" and then grab you by the hand to lead you somewhere. This is almost always a prelude to a prank. To test the teen's intentions, simply resist being led away and look for her response. If she insists that you follow her, prepare yourself for an imminent prank. FYI: The person who says, "I want to show you something" is almost certainly not the instigator of the prank. She's merely the "go get her and bring her in here" accomplice.

10. There will be times when you need to lay down the law. For trips and retreats, set the tone in advance of the trip and on the first day. Kids will generally follow your lead. If you think pranks will distract you from what you're hoping to accomplish on the retreat, tell your kids in advance that pranks aren't allowed. Then have your adult helpers confiscate any questionable materials for the duration of the trip. Remember, feeling safe is an important element as kids grow in their relationships with God. If they're looking over their shoulders all weekend, expecting to be victimized by a prank, they're not feeling safe.

11. Don't neglect "Yucknights." Plan a few events during the year in which kids can cut loose and get messy.

THE ANATOMY OF A TEEN PRANK

Step 1: The Set-Up

To pull off a prank, there's a certain amount of preparatory work that must take place. Whether it involves filling up water balloons, turning on the hose, retrieving duct tape from a car, or climbing onto the church roof, the set-up usually happens in secret and generally takes a few minutes. You'll likely never know anything is being set up unless you have a small youth group, and all your kids disappear for a short time. Even the best youth pastors usually don't know the set-up is happening. Your only hope is for a loyal home-school student to turn Benedict Arnold on the rest of the kids (generally from sheer guilt) and let you in on the plot.

Step 2: Positioning

The set-up is complete, and the kids are ready to execute the prank. This is where you become involved. The prank plotters will ask you to move. They know better than to throw their arsenal of water balloons at you inside the church gym, so they need you to go to them.

Step 3: Execution

If your "prankin-sense" isn't going off at this point, you may be a goner. This is where the shaving cream, water balloons, toothpaste, toilet paper, and duct tape roll like a mighty river.

How to Drive Off a Student to Another Youth Group

1. Take the student's name off your mailing list.

2. Send the kid postcards from other youth pastors, inviting her to attend the other churches' youth functions.

3. Do a series on being ecumenical. Encourage all of your kids to visit another church youth group for the next month. Then, later that night, call all the kids except your problem child and tell them you were only kidding.

4. When the kid misbehaves say, "We don't do that kind of thing at this church...but the church down the street does!"

5. Give her brochures to another church's youth ministry and say, "I just happened upon these flyers for this really cool youth program, and I thought about you when I saw them."

6. Invite another church's youth pastor to go to the kid's school with you for lunch. Then introduce the youth pastor to your problem child by saying, "This is the best youth pastor in the city for kids like you."

7. Give her an anonymous scholarship to another church's summer camp.

8. Leave her anonymous notes that say things like, "You're a really great kid, and God loves you, but he will love you more if you go to church down the street."

9. Toilet-paper the church inside and out. Then spray-paint the kid's name all over the lawn. Let the pastor get rid of her for you.

10. Ask her, "What can I do to help you not come here anymore?"

How to Talk Out of Both Sides of Your Mouth

1. Take kids to feed the hungry in your city...then kick off your fall programming with "the world's largest food fight."

2. Talk about God's love for creation...then use paper for your talk outline, the group game, the bulletin, the calendar, and photocopies for your kids.

3. Tell kids they're leaders...then plan and lead everything for them.

4. Emphasize to kids the importance of being in a small group...then refuse to join one yourself.

5. Tell kids about the importance of making friends with people who don't follow Jesus...then surround yourself with friends from the church.

6. Tell kids about the importance of priorities...then work 60 hours a week and let your family suffer.

7. Tell kids about the importance of going to "big church"...then avoid it yourself at all costs.

8. Tell kids to honor their father and mother...then crack jokes about parents in private and public conversations.

9. Tell kids about the evils of consumerism and how the world is manipulating them with advertising to get them to buy stuff...then put a Coke machine in your youth room and create a four-color calendar for youth events on which you write things like, "All your

friends will be there!" and "Don't be the one who misses out!"

10. Tell kids that church is about relationships...then fill your ministry with programs.

11. Tell your congregation it's important for students to have consistent adults of all ages involved in their lives...then campaign to get a new youth building detached from the existing facility.

How to Listen

Listening will get you further in youth ministry than talking. (Read that last line again in case you weren't paying attention.) Hearing someone is different from listening to them.

Listening is especially important for youth pastors, many of whom have ears damaged by bad music being blasted from bad sound systems. As a general rule, younger youth pastors are good at hearing, but not so great at listening. Older youth pastors are good at listening, but not so great at hearing.

Regardless of which category you fall into, here are some tips for better listening.

1. Take the ear bud headphones out of your ears.

2. Close your eyes and repeat this phrase to yourself three times: "Listening will get me further in youth ministry than talking."

3. Say this: "What can I help you with today?"

4. Close your mouth.

5. Keep it closed.

6. Ask yourself the question, "What is this person trying to tell me?"

7. Keep your mouth closed some more.

8. Ignore the squirrel outside the window.

9. Remember what the other person is saying.

10. Ask a question directly related to what the other person is saying. But do not give advice.

11. Keep that mouth closed.

12. Continue to ignore the squirrel outside.

13. Put down the thing you're fidgeting with.

14. Stop daydreaming.

15. Always keep gas in.

16. Repeat what you think the person is saying. Start with, "If I hear you correctly, you're saying..."

17. Pay attention to the person's answer.

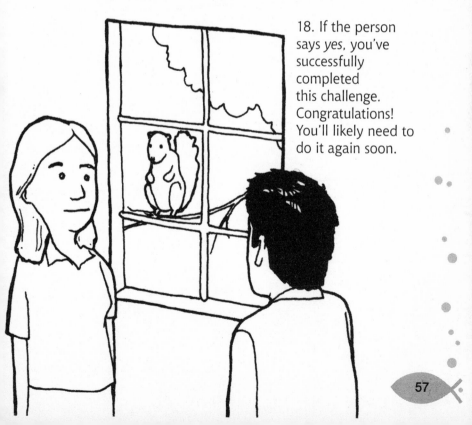

18. If the person says *yes*, you've successfully completed this challenge. Congratulations! You'll likely need to do it again soon.

Section 3:

JUMPING THROUGH HOOPS

How to Survive a Staff Meeting

Got an upcoming meeting that you're dreading? Liven up the proceedings with a stealth game of BINGO. Play by yourself or with other like-minded staff members. Simply choose the BINGO card that best fits your church (Pentecostal, Baptist, Progressive, Emerging, or Mainline). Every time you hear one of the words on your card, cover that square. When you cover an entire row (vertically, horizontally, or diagonally), you know what to do. (You'll notice that each card has a Free Space, which contains the word most likely to be uttered in your meeting.)

PENTECOSTAL STAFF MEETING

B	I	N	G	O
Manifest	Private jet	Word of knowledge	Holiness	Armani
un-	Offering	Sister	Felt	Seed
Revelation	Prophecy	**FREE** Anointing	The world	Pluralism
Fire	Hell	The Devil	Spirit-filled	Charisma
Broadcast	Tour	Power	Apostolic	Revival

BAPTIST STAFF MEETING

BINGO

Sin	Saved	Steeple	Disney	Worldly
Purpose-driven	Family life center	Hell	Brother	Mention of church down the street
Liberal	Sinner	**FREE** Baptist (no one talks about themselves as much)	Building program	Sunday school
Homo-sexual	Sin	Faith and message	Missionaries speaking in tongues	Hell
Potluck	Convention	Liberty	The Word of God	America

PROGRESSIVE CHURCH STAFF MEETING

$$B \quad I \quad N \quad G \quad O$$

Contemporary	Culture	Life stage	Perception	World-class
State-of-the-art	Vision	Initiative	Equip	Video venue
Live feed on the T1 line	Lumens	**FREE** Leader	.tv	Catalyst
Lighting director	Inspire	Viral	J-Crew	Set (in reference to the music)
Set (in reference to the stage background)	Design	Campus	Values	WWASD? What would Andy Stanley do?

EMERGING CHURCH STAFF MEETING

BINGO

Village	Ecclesi-ology	Blog	Conver-sation	System
Organic	Cohort	Hemp	Friend	Volf
Liturgy	Coffee	**FREE** Community	Rhythm	Whole
Dialogue	Vibe	Kingdom of God	Environ-ment	Wright
Podcast	Missional	Ethos	Home	Creed

MAINLINE CHURCH STAFF MEETING

BINGO

Service	Committee	Trustee	Endow-ment	Funeral
Organist	Rite	Justice	Robe	Choir
Memorial carpet	Building	**FREE** Calendar	Stained (glass or carpet)	Potluck
Discipline	Tradition	Picnic	Hospital visitation	Membership
Chapel	Coordi-nator	Education	Alarm	Altar

How to Prevent Spelling Mistakes in Your Documents

A BRIEF HISTORY OF SPELLING IN YOUTH MINISTRY

In the history of youth ministry, there have only been four documents (printed and delivered) that were free of spelling errors.

In 1987 Dick Read of Tulsa, Oklahoma, used a typewriter and state-of-the-art cut-and-paste technology (clear tape and scissors on a photo copier) to produce a document free of spelling errors. This is the only known error-free newsletter to have been generated by a youth pastor.

In 1999 Scott French, a youth pastor from Buffalo, New York, drafted a letter to parents that didn't contain a single misspelled word. It was a close call, though. The document almost went out with an invitation for moms and dads to attend "Parents Desert on the night of Febuary forth." Scott's wife Rondi saw the document and made the corrections without Scott's knowing—and history was made.

On March 3, 2004, Denise McKinney sent an email that was error free. It contained six words.

On November 7, 2008, Mike Steele sent a text message that was completely void of actual words, and thus, technically, was spelled correctly. Here is a transcript of that message:

WU? HIG? GAS?

IHTFP

U-L 2

GFYMF

CUNS

LY4E

YIC

MS

His intention was to write:

> *What's up? How's it going? Got a second?*
>
> *I have truly found paradise.*
>
> *You will, too.*
>
> *God forgives you, my friends.*
>
> *See you in school.*
>
> *Love you forever.*
>
> *Yours in Christ,*
>
> *Mike Steele*

Unfortunately, what Mike thought was an encouraging note to his students about a relationship with Christ was interpreted as a profanity-laced tirade that got him fired.

HOW TO PREVENT SPELLING MISTAKES

1. Pad your annual youth ministry budget by $50,000 and hire a full-time proofreader.

2. Before you send anything out, post every piece of correspondence on a Web site and let all the anal-retentive grammarian flamers in cyberspace tell you exactly what's wrong with it.

3. Use Spell Check.

How to Dig a Mud Pit

1. Select a desirable location. You'll need a site with access to water. The pit will be approximately 30 feet by 20 feet.
   a. Specifications for a high-quality mud pit location:
      • The area should be relatively flat.
      • The area should not be too rocky. (Kids will be running barefoot and diving.)
      • The area should be free of underground utilities such as electricity, sewage, and gas.
      • The area should be near a lake or pond (not as a source of water, but as a place to jump in to clean up).
   b. Less-than-ideal locations for a mud pit:
      • Sites with rocky or clay soil
      • Sloped surfaces, such the side of a hill
      • Beaches
      • The senior pastor's front yard
      • Indoors
      • Public parks
      • Deserts, mesas, and riverbeds
      • Any site that requires the use of buckets
      • Snake- or alligator-infested swamps and marshes

2. Borrow the following equipment:
      • 300 to 600 feet of hose
      • A rototiller[3] with extra gas
      • One good pair of leather work gloves

3. Soften the ground by running water on the site for at least eight hours. Move the hose every 90 minutes to ensure maximum coverage.

---

[3] You may substitute a 12-ton 2005 Caterpillar 446D backhoe loader with optional pilot-operated joystick controls, self-leveling enhancements, and return-to-dig system.

4. Use the rototiller to dig up the earth. This is hard work and will take up to six hours to finish. Bring a buddy and take turns.

5. Take care not to overheat. Wear sunscreen and a hat to keep cool.

6. Reflect back on your call to ministry and how, in that moment, you were convinced that God was calling you make a real difference in the world.

Recipe for mud: Find dirt and add water.

Tip: If you purchase dirt for your mud pit, be sure to buy clean dirt. "Clean dirt" sounds like an oxymoron—until you find out what dirty dirt is. Clean dirt is free of refuse and debris. We suggest purchasing clean dirt, unless you want to change the name of Mud Pit Night to Guano Night.

How to Promote a Rock Concert

Some people in your congregation believe that holding a rock concert is the best possible way to get kids closer to Jesus. That's good news for you. If the whole ministry thing doesn't work out for you, you can always get a gig as a concert promoter. In the meantime, there are certain things you need to know about deepening your students' spiritual lives through guitar solos, drum risers, and dry ice.

Of course, if you have *really* spiritual kids, they won't want anything to do with rock concerts. In that case, you should consider hosting a "worship event," complete with a great worship leader—or "lead worshiper." The worship leader you choose must be *real*. "Real," in this case, means available to hang out after the show and sign autographs.

Regardless of the direction you choose to go, here are some important things to know about promoting a rock concert or worship event.

1. Pick a good band that you can afford.

2. Print tickets.

3. Spend lots of money on promotion. Promotion is the key to outreach. Make sure you put flyers in all the Christian bookstores in your area. And make sure that your local Christian radio stations know about it. This is the standard method churches use to reach out to lost people in their city. After all, lost people like Christian music, right?

4. Remember, marketing is the modern way to evangelize.

5. Call other youth pastors in your area and send flyers to their churches. Pretend to be best friends with your colleagues—the ones you ignore the other 10 months of the year—as you try to convince them to come to your event.

How to Return a Phone Call

Youth pastors are often stereotyped as gadget junkies who are able to run obscure computer software, set up amazingly complex sound systems, and operate the latest cell phones and PDAs with no problem. For all that technical know-how, though, youth pastors are notorious for not returning phone calls.

Even if you don't mind being labeled unreliable or irresponsible, please take the time to start returning your calls. Do it for your fellow youth workers. You're giving us all a bad name.

If it's been a while since you returned a call, here's a quick refresher course.

Step 1

When checking your voice mail, write down the name and number of the person who called on a piece of paper that you won't lose. Do the same thing for each call.

Step 2

Pick up the phone.

Step 3

Listen for a dial tone. (It's a long, continuous note.) If you can't hear a dial tone, try flipping the phone around.

Step 4

Look for a grouping of numbers that resembles this:

Step 5

Refer to the paper with the phone number on it. Dial each number in order, from left to right.

Step 6

Listen for the phone to ring on the other end.

Step 7

When the person answers the phone, quickly look at the paper to see the name of the person you called.

Step 8

The rest should come naturally to you.

How to Turn Down an Invitation

Youth pastors get invited to do a lot of things. Unfortunately, you can't say "yes" to everything. So how do you say "no" to an invitation without creating all kinds of weird awkwardness? You use a form letter!

Here's an easy-to-use form for declining an invitation. Feel free to photocopy it, check the appropriate boxes, and send it to the person who invited you.

Thanks for the invitation to...

___ breakfast/lunch/dinner

___ lead VBS

___ lead a small group

___ preach

___ cheat on my spouse

___ leave my position

___ baptize your pet

___ fix your kid

___ write a recommendation

___ listen to you complain

___ lead the staff devotional

___ the movie

___ church

___ a date

___ sing in the choir

___ sing a solo

___ the birthday party

___ the anniversary party

___ donate

___ dance

___ chaperone

___ work for you

___ the benefit for _____

___ Bible study

___ be your youth pastor

___ be your pastor

___ usher

___ organize the Women's Ministry

___ write an article for the bulletin

As it turns out, I already have plans to...

___ be on vacation

___ lead a youth activity

___ wash my hair

___ lose my hair

___ grow old by myself

___ sleep

___ play video games

___ go out

___ skydive

___ eat

___ love Jesus in another way

___ hang myself from my ankles

___ go hunting and kill some animals

___ ignore poverty and starving children

___ give to the needs of others

___ have "me time"

___ spend time away from you

___ wax my back

___ pull my fingernails out one at a time with pliers

___ sing

___ party

___ see that movie with someone else

___ be disciplined by the church

___ work out my personal demons (*Get out!!!*)

___ lose my voice

___ be injured

___ walk across the country

I'd rather...

___ take a rain-check

___ not do it

___ die like a disciple

___ keep my issues to myself, thanks

___ you keep your issues to yourself

___ eat a rhino

___ see a New Kids on the Block reunion concert

Maybe...

___ another time?

___ next time?

___ later that day?

___ you'll stop asking me?

___ never?

___ I'll die before then?

___ hell will freeze over?

___ Jesus will come back?

___ the church will discipline me?

Salutation

___ Thanks anyway,

___ Sincerely,

___ Go to blazes,

___ Hoping you'll stop talking to me,

___ Godspeed,

___ Your friend,

___ Your enemy,

___ Your youth pastor,

___ Your pastor,

___ Yours truly,

_____

(Sign your name here)

How to Make a List

It's not that youth workers have poor memories. It's just that the amount of information youth workers have to work with is so immense that sometimes forgetfulness is unavoidable. That's why lists are a youth worker's best friend. List-making can reduce the stress in your life. Lists can keep you from being consumed with remembering things. Here are some tips for effective list-making.

1. Get something to write on that you can carry with you.

2. Write down phone calls you need to return (along with the phone numbers, if possible), conversations you need to have, and items you need to purchase.

3. If it's helpful, write a deadline next to urgent items on the list.

4. Refer to your list often.

5. Do the things on your list.

6. Mark items off as you accomplish them.

TO DO LIST

TASK	DUE
X Call Dan 555-6767	TODAY
— Call Brenda 555-4545	MONDAY
— Buy 5 lbs. of Flour	SUNDAY
— Buy 15 ft. of medical tubing	SUNDAY
X Buy glow in the dark masking tape	WEDNESDAY
— Clean up toilet paper @ house	TODAY
— Wash car / remove shoe polish	TODAY
— Buy a bunch of CD's I'll never use	TODAY
— Pick up tux for the opera	TUESDAY

How to Get Other Youth Workers to Stop Sending You Email Forwards

1. First, it's important to realize that the offending youth worker loves you and doesn't realize how utterly annoying his forwards are.

2. It's also important to note that while the forwards he sends you are sappy, theologically inept, lame, and often completely made-up trash, they're evidently deeply meaningful and moving to him. He sends them to inspire you along in your faith. Remember this when you crush him.

3. Program your email software so that it directs the offending youth worker's email messages to a particular folder. Label it with a file name such as "Junk" or the ever-subtle "File #13." It's important to occasionally skim the contents of this folder in case your youth worker friend ever sends you something of value. Of course, that's not very likely, as people who have time to read and pass on a large volume of email forwards rarely contribute anything meaningful to the world.

4. After creating the "File #13" folder in your inbox, wait for the right moment to act. You're waiting for a Snopes-able forward. (Snopes.com is a Web site that specializes in debunking rumors and questionable "news" often found in email forwards. A Snopes-able email won't be a touching poem about footprints in the sand. It will be an alarming news flash about a child with cancer who's being mistreated or a credit card company that's preparing to issue the mark of the beast. You'll know it when you see it.) When you get it, look up the information on snopes.com, which

will verify it as "Fact" or "False." Wait for a "False" confirmation.

5. Once you receive the confirmation, hit "Reply All" and type the following statement:

> Hello everyone,
>
> You might be interested to know that the information in this email is false. Go to snopes.com for more info. [Include link here.]
>
> As leaders in the church, let's please be more careful about what we send out to people.
>
> Signed,
>
> [Insert your name.]

6. This should stop the unwanted forwards.

How to Plagiarize for Jesus

God certainly doesn't expect you to develop and share meaningful insights based only on your personal prayer time, Bible study, life experiences, and relationship with Jesus. That's why plagiarism is such an important aspect of pastoral work. Whether you're writing a paper for school, trying to come up with a strong sermon series, or creating a vision statement, there's no need to spend your time actually thinking through who you are, who God is, and what he wants for the world through you. Not when you can plagiarize your way to spiritual leadership.

You'll find that symbols like © or ™ usually indicate that something is worth plagiarizing. Of course, you'll also find that there's an element of society that views plagiarism as a bad thing.

Take the odd person[4] who wrote the definition for *plagiarize* in the Merriam-Webster Dictionary (*www.merriam-Webster.com/ dictionary/plagiarize*).[5] Just read this completely biased view:

> : to steal and pass off the ideas or words of another as one's own; use another's production without crediting the source

> : to commit literary theft; present as new and original an idea or product derived from an existing source

Obviously that person didn't wake up on the right side of the bed or eat his Alpha-Bits the morning he wrote that. And what kind of name is *Merriam*, anyway?[6]

---

[4] Who writes dictionaries anyway?

[5] I only cite my source here because my editor made me. Otherwise I wouldn't do it, because God breathed in me the same definition.

[6] Noah Webster wrote the original dictionary. *Noah* is a strong biblical name. But once those Merriams (from Massachusetts, no less) took over the dictionary

As a Christian, your first response when you read that definition may be to conclude that it's morally wrong to use someone else's material because you're too lazy to come up with something of your own. And you may see that as an obstacle to your own future as a plagiarist.

But that response would be wrong. Because you, as a Christian, have an out. A wild card: Divine revelation.[7]

If God spoke something to one person, can he not speak it to someone else? The Holy Spirit spoke to Paul and Peter separately, but essentially told them the same thing. Sure, it wasn't a word-for-word match. But is it too much of a stretch to say that if God tells Rick Warren, Bill Hybels, or Rob Bell something, you can't receive the same revelation, word for word?

WHEN ACCUSED OF PLAGIARISM

1. Deny. Deny. Deny. Claim inspiration and specific revelation. Very. Specific. Revelation.

2. Tell the story of being alone in the coffee shop when God spoke to you so clearly, you knew in that moment you had to share the information. (It's best to leave out any mention of the book or MP3 file God used to inspire you.)

3. ~~If~~ When the powers that be punish you for plagiarism, consider yourself among the great martyrs for God.

---

from the good, conservatively named Webster, I'm sure they changed the definition of many words.

[7] Unless you're a liberal and don't believe God reveals himself to people like that.

NOTE TO ULTRA-CONSERVATIVE FUNDAMENTALISTS

Chances are, you believe everything you say is God's Word anyway, so this entire chapter may not be of any real use to you.

Section 4:

BEING ALL THAT YOU CAN BE

How to Know When It's Time to Leave

1. The senior pastor begins referring to you as the "interim youth pastor."

2. The teens in your ministry forward you Web sites of youth pastor job listings and encourage you to check them out.

3. Your key no longer opens your office door.

4. You overhear the church receptionist telling a caller, "No, we don't currently have a youth pastor."

5. You find your church and position listed on the online youth pastor job board.

6. You open your office door and find a rabid 165-pound rottweiler waiting for you.

7. Your kids organize a competing Bible study down the hall from your Bible study on Wednesday nights.

8. You begin to receive phone calls in the middle of the night from scary voices that sound like members of your elder board talking through a towel, saying, "Your eschatology is wrong, and your hermeneutical lens is heretical!"

9. Your senior pastor mutters, "Get behind me, Satan," every time he sees you.

10. Your students' parents create a Web site called *www. getridofouryouthpastor.com*.

11. The ex-gang member in your youth group confesses that the other kids aren't raising funds for a mission trip, but to pay for the $3,000 hit on you.

12. You complain of a headache, and a youth worker rushes over to offer you unusual white pills that have "Tylenol" written in red marker across them.

13. During paintball, both teams shoot at you.

14. You pull back the covers of your bed and find the head of a chubby bunny.

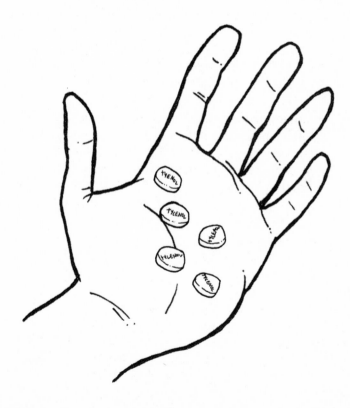

How to Crash and Burn as a Youth Pastor in Less Than Five Years

1. Believe that you're a rock star—THE youth ministry expert in the church.

2. Take responsibility for everything that happens to, with, and for the kids in your church.

3. If you really want a different vocation in a few years, completely ignore theology and its role in what you do week in and week out.

4. Spend time regularly in relationship-building and one-on-one prayer with someone of the opposite gender.

5. Exclude, alienate, talk against, and look down on your students' parents. Never do anything that actually supports parents in their ministry to their children.

6. Send anonymous hate mail to your pastor from your church computer.

7. Believe you have all the resources you need to lead a youth ministry at the age of 25. It's also helpful to believe that 20-somethings hold the most important and effective gifts for youth ministry.

8. Believe that you're a wiser and more gifted leader than your pastor.

9. Never take a vacation or days off.

10. Feel surprised every time something goes wrong, because you believe there will actually be a time when everything always goes smoothly.

How to Make Friends in a New City

Moving to a new city for a ministry position can be difficult. But if you find yourself in that position, it's vital that you make socializing in your new surroundings a priority. Making friends outside the church is important for your spiritual and emotional health. Quite simply, if you don't have friends your own age, something is wrong. Here are some ideas for meeting people in a new town.

1. Join a softball league.

2. Invite neighbors over once a month for a meal.

3. Get a locker at a local cigar bar.

4. Coach soccer, football, volleyball, softball, or baseball at a local school. Meet parents.

5. Join a book club at the local bookstore or library.

6. Start a book club at the local bookstore or library.

7. Go to local small theater and concert venues.

8. Take a class that interests you at the local junior college.

9. Talk to people at the gym while you work out.

10. Frequent a local coffee shop and learn people's names.

11. Help build a Habitat House with people who aren't from your church.

12. Volunteer at a local ministry that serves the poor.

13. Start a punk rock band.

14. Start a men's/women's group in your church with people who are older than you.

15. Sign up for a bus trip to a pro sports game.

16. Start a side business doing something you love 10 hours a week.

17. Go for walks in the park.

18. Check your breath to make sure you aren't running people off.

19. Change to a stronger deodorant.

20. Get a hobby and connect with locals who do what you love.

21. Join a drum circle.

22. Connect with local alumni of schools you attended.

23. Join an online community, as well as local community groups.

24. Learn to square dance.

25. Take your new neighbors a bundt cake.

26. Get your neighbors to come over and play poker every couple of months.

27. Become head of the neighborhood watch.

28. Use some of the creativity that comes naturally for youth programming for your own life.

How to Use the Guy Handshake-Hug Combo

As literally as we in the church take the apostle Paul, we have no problem skipping over Romans 16:16. Instead of the recommended kiss to greet one another, men of the church have developed the Guy Handshake-Hug Combo. The GHHC says, "Friends don't shake hands—friends hug...but not with both hands."

Here's the proper way to employ the Guy Handshake-Hug. Follow these instructions very carefully.

1. As you approach the other individual, start the conversation.

2. Extend your right hand for the handshake. Use a firm grip.

3. Don't let go of the handshake.

4. Extend your left hand around to the back of the person you're greeting.

5. Slap high, near the shoulder blades—never low on the back or near the belt.

6. Turn your head to the left to avoid facial contact or the awkward moment when you don't know which side your head should go and onlookers think the two of you might kiss.

7. Keep talking.

8. Slap three times. Slap. Do not pat. Patting connotes weakness. Slap. The harder you slap, the manlier you are.

9. Each slap represents one word in the Evangelical Guy Code Book. Three slaps during the Guy Handshake-Hug Combo says, "I'm...not...gay."

10. Never, ever touch cheeks to another man.

11. Never, ever rest your head on the shoulder of another man.

12. And absolutely never, ever cry on another man's shoulder. Remember Ed Norton and Meat Loaf in *Fight Club*?

13. After the three slaps, wait a fraction of a second before pulling away. Pulling away too quickly sends a similar vibe to patting the other person's back.

14. Keep talking.

15. Pull back from the hug maneuver and establish proper distance for talking face to face.

16. Let go of the handshake. Be careful to release the entire hand simultaneously. Never let one finger linger longer than the others.

17. Keep talking.

18. The move is complete. Congratulations on implementing a successful GHHC.

APPROPRIATE USES OF THE GHHC

1. When you greet a friend for the first time that day.

2. When you're saying goodbye after a conversation in which you gave the GHHC as a greeting or in which you felt a friend connection with the guy you're talking to.

INAPPROPRIATE USES OF THE GHHC

1. In the middle of a conversation

2. In the middle of a meal

3. In the middle of a double date

4. In the middle of anything

How to Make the Most of a National Youth Workers Convention

HOW TO PICK THE CITY

1. Mount a map of the United States on your wall. Put a pushpin in your hometown. Then put pushpins in the locations of the various national conventions.

2. Use the following criteria for picking the city:
   a. Which city is closest to you? Carefully calculate the distance in miles. Don't round the number up or down.
   b. Which city is most cost-effective? Carefully calculate the travel cost to each city. Include hotel, food, and miscellaneous expenses in your total.
   c. To which city can you bring other volunteers? If you drive, you can save money and bring additional volunteers.
   d. Which city has the best lineup of speakers and artists? Seeing a speaker who's important to you and speaks to your soul is critical.
   e. Which city has the best weather/beaches/attractions/fun? Visit an online concert ticket broker to see where your favorite band will be playing.

3. After you've diligently worked through each of these variables, go with the city you chose for "e."

IF YOU BRING A TEAM...

1. Wear matching T-shirts every day. Make sure they have bright, neon colors.

2. Print a memorable phrase on your shirts, such as...
   - Body by Hagee
   - They will know we are Christians by our T-Shirts
   - We love our youth pastor
   - My pastor can beat up your pastor
   - Dainty
   - First Church: Where everyone knows your name and all the other details of your life
   - Our choir could eat your choir for lunch
   - Hope: We don't have much of it, but tomorrow can't be much worse than yesterday
   - First Church of Reason
   - (On the front) Single and Pentecostal (On the back) Wanna speak in tongues?

3. Encourage team members to pose the following questions and comments to the convention leaders every time they see them:
   - "When does dc Talk play again?"
   - "Nice pants."
   - "I'd like to see more Bible in the seminars."
   - "Was your goatee featured in *Goatee Weekly*?"
   - "When you're done with those fancy lights, can I have them?"
   - "When are we doing the convention in [your town]?"
   - "Hey, Butch, where's Cassidy?"
   - "Can you sing happy birthday to my friend? No, not from the stage. Right now."

HOW TO MAKE THE MOST OF THE EXHIBIT HALL

1. Pack an extra suitcase for freebies.

2. Enter the ~~Den of Thieves~~ Exhibit Hall. Pick up a brochure from the first big exhibit you see. Make sure the brochure contains that particular company's mailing address, including zip code.

3. Exit the Exhibit Hall and transfer the address from the brochure to a blank piece of paper. Now you're ready to get free stuff. (Some exhibitors require you to fill out information cards to get your free stuff. If that happens, pull out the piece of paper and write down the address that's on it.)

4. Re-enter the Exhibit Hall with the sheet of paper.

5. Give exhibitors the bogus address and collect free stuff.

How to Be a Postmodern Youth Pastor

1. Talk more about ministry ideas, philosophy, and models than about Jesus. Talk about relevance so much that you become irrelevant. If people are going to take you seriously as a postmodern youth pastor, you need to be able to talk the talk.

2. During sermons, use hushed, airy, and serious tones to convey passion and intensity. Everyone knows that postmodern youth pastors are more real than modern pastors. The best way to be perceived as real is to have moments in your sermons where your tone is intense, conveying passion. If you can make yourself sound like you might cry at any moment, that will work, too.

3. Use words such as *deconstruction, meta-narrative, post-foundational*, and *colonialism*.

4. Attach the prefix *re* to as many words as possible: *ReImagine. ReThink. ReEmerge. ReGurgitate.*

5. Spend a significant amount of time publicly telling others what's wrong with other churches and pastors.

6. Cuss frequently during your sermons.

7. Place lava lamps on your end tables.

8. Throw all your money into sound equipment, advertising (about how different your church is), and enough candles to send your congregation into allergy-induced comas.

9. Let yourself become an arrogant jerk.

10. Show R-rated movie clips in your worship services.

11. Make up for what you lack in character with goatee length.

12. Be completely misunderstood with characterizations such as the ones listed above.

How to Support the Youth Worker Down the Street

Youth pastors must support each other. Finding true friends—especially ones in ministry—is difficult. Being there for a peer is what Jesus' community is all about. Let's take a look at the dynamic using the following case study.

Denny is a youth pastor in a large church in your community. Denny is your friend. You've worked together on local youth events. You've confided in him often and sought his advice. Today he called and asked to meet with you. He needs someone to talk to. Here's how you can support Denny:

1. Arrange to meet him at a local coffee shop not frequented by church members.

2. Pray for Denny on the way to your meeting.

3. Greet him with the Guy Handshake-Hug Combo.

4. Buy him a cup of coffee. Offer dessert, but not in a convincing tone.

5. Grab a couple of comfy chairs.

6. Give him your full attention. Listen carefully. Take mental notes.

7. Ask questions.

8. Suggest a youth ministry consultant who could help.

9. Tell him you're genuinely sorry that he's going to resign.

10. Pray for him.

11. Give him the Guy Handshake-Hug Combo as you leave.

12. Pray for him on the way back to your office.

13. Get on your computer and send him an encouraging email.

14. Stay on your computer and brush up your resume.

15. When Denny resigns, send your resume immediately.

How to Stay Out of Touch with the Real World

1. Avoid local artists and the venues in which they display or perform their art.

2. Avoid places that serve alcohol and the people who frequent them.

3. Avoid downtown and stay in the suburbs.

4. Hang out only with people like you—same race, same age, same marital status, same number of children, same socioeconomic status.

5. Hang out only with kids.

6. Spend time only with people in your church.

7. Read only Christian books.

8. Think and talk only about church stuff.

9. Listen to Christian music exclusively.

10. Travel as little as possible.

11. Think of yourself first and foremost as a pastor.

12. Fill up your life with activities.

13. Develop a discipline of never asking people hard questions that might reveal how they're really doing.

14. Enjoy porn—often.

15. Enjoy podcasts and books by Christian leadership gurus—often.

16. Objectify people as cogs that you use to make your world go round.

17. Talk about being real and authentic, but never open up yourself emotionally.

18. Cut off all contact with your actual neighbors. Keep it to a smile and a wave.

19. Avoid topics that make you think or ask questions.

20. Diminish the opinions and thoughts of your spouse.

How to Have Fun in the Hotel Elevator at a Youth Workers Convention

Remember, for the duration of a youth conference, normal rules governing social interaction and decorum don't apply! The name of the game is fun, fun, fun. Here are some tips for transforming a mundane elevator ride with strangers into something memorable.

1. Ask people if they like your pants.

2. Yell out the floor numbers as they pass. When you reach your desired floor, clap, cheer, and high-five everyone in the elevator.

3. Sit on the floor and sing the *Barney* theme song. Then giggle to yourself.

4. Bark.

5. When the doors open, announce, "Third floor: Ladies lingerie."

6. Do a handstand.

7. Repeat the following to yourself in your normal voice: "No! I'm not going to do it! I'm a good boy/girl, and youth workers are nice people!"

8. Get a dog leash. When someone new gets on the elevator, hold the leash, get on your hands and knees, and look down the crack in the door. In a panicked voice, yell, "I'm sorry, Fe-Fe! I thought you could make it over the crack!"

9. Spill some water in the corner of the elevator. Stand there, facing the wall, and repeat, "I thought I could hold it! I thought I could hold it!"

10. Jump up and down.

11. If it's a glass elevator, press yourself against the window and say, "I'm flying!"

12. Enter the elevator on the first floor, then say, "Behold I am with you always, even unto the end of the age." Then ascend to your room.

13. Sit on the floor.

14. Spray water all over your face and pretend that it's sweat. As people get on the elevator, wipe your brow and announce breathlessly, "This is a killer workout!"

15. After the doors close, say, "I'm glad you all could make it to the Critical Concerns Course on How to Minister to Teenage Claustrophobics."

16. Face and stare at another person without blinking for the entire elevator ride.

How to Be a Professional Christian

If you spend more than a few years in youth ministry, it's easy to get confused about your spiritual life. Many church leaders don't even know they're confused. If you can't tell the difference between You: The Adult Person and You: The Youth Pastor, then you may have become a professional Christian. Here are some characteristics to look for:

1. Every time you read your Bible, you think to yourself, *This will make a great lesson for the next youth program.*

2. You pray only before meals, before staff meetings, and before and after youth group.

3. You emphasize to your students the importance of community, but you don't create space for community in your own life.

4. You emphasize to your students the importance of reaching out to their friends, but you don't develop relationships with people your own age or reach out to other adults.

5. You use the excuse that your students are your community and mission field—and really believe it.

6. When watching an enjoyable TV show or a movie, your first thought is, *This will make a great clip for a lesson.*

If any of these characteristics apply to you, then chances are you're a professional Christian, and you need help immediately.

How to Recover from Being a Professional Christian

1. Admit you're a professional Christian. Tell someone who's older, wiser, and preferably not employed at a church.

2. Find a spiritual director.

3. Resist the urge to become a spiritual director yourself. I know it sounds cool, but you need to help yourself first.

4. Keep looking. You'll probably discover that spiritual directors are hard to find in a world filled with pastors, ministers, and lead pastors.

5. Plan ahead.
   - Schedule your days off months in advance.
   - Schedule a personal silent retreat quarterly. (Use vacation time, if you need to.)
   - Plan for work-related study at the church or Coffee Shop A.
   - Plan for personal study at home or anywhere else *but* Coffee Shop A.
   - Use a different Bible for your work-related study.
   - Suggest a sabbatical policy for pastors in your church, giving them three months off every seven years—in addition to vacation time. (The person who tells you "no" probably isn't a spiritual director.)

6. Use a fixed-hour prayer discipline.

7. Use the lectionary for your teaching. This will keep you from wanting to use everything you read in your personal time.

8. Meet with your spiritual director regularly.

9. Enjoy movies and TV shows. Resist the urge to use them for youth programming.

HOW TO IDENTIFY A SPIRITUAL DIRECTOR

1. The person spends a lot of time praying and being quiet. The person may use terms such as *daily offices, solitude, pilgrimage,* and *spiritual disciplines.*

2. The person likely intimidates you a bit.

3. The person isn't looking to give you advice.

4. The person asks great questions that God uses to reveal things to you.

5. The person probably isn't trained in spiritual direction (but might be).

	Lead Pastor	**Spiritual Director**
Likely to mention in a conversation ...	Leadership, vision, church, strategy	Prayer, disciplines, silence, rhythm
Loves to ...	Talk	Listen
Talks about ...	Doing	Being
Believes his/ her role in conversation is to ...	Give advice	Ask questions
Has a deep desire to ...	Grow a church	Nurture people

Things They Don't Teach You as a Youth Ministry Major

1. How to tie a thousand water balloons without getting a blister.

2. How to remove shaving cream from the ceiling.

3. How to paint ceiling tiles in the youth room to make them actually look good.

4. How to actually be a pastor.

5. Theology.

6. What a fire code is and why running 35 extension cords through the drop ceiling in the youth room is a violation.

7. That your youth ministry major will impress your adult friends almost as much as your art minor does.

8. How to get candle wax out of Sister Mary Martha's Memorial Carpet in the church parlor.

9. Discernment.

10. How to deal with the passive-aggressive executive at Walco who thinks he should be the youth pastor.

APPENDIX

Dear (insert name of complainer),

I just received your email this morning when I got into the office. First, I must say that I appreciate your colorful use of the English language. I am delighted by your frequent use of the phrase "them kids." And I was riveted by your description of the youth group as "showen no respect buy trashin the churches van." [Such niceties set a convivial tone for the letter. Who doesn't appreciate a compliment? If the writer's literary achievements are duly noted, he may be more likely to continue reading your reply.]

I also appreciate that you chose not to gossip and came directly to me with your issue, thus living out the principles of Matthew 18. [Okay, look, this is a church. No one ever goes directly to the person he has an issue with. I've found the preceding passive-aggressive language is helpful both in making the complainer feel guilty and share the blame for bad behavior. Of course, such a reply is completely unbiblical. But this is church. If you're going to work here, you're going to need some chops.]

Of course, I want to meet personally with you ASAP so that we can discuss this urgent and important matter and resolve it quickly.

In Christ,

(insert your name)

Thanks for the invitation to...

___ breakfast/lunch/dinner
___ lead VBS
___ lead a small group
___ preach
___ cheat on my spouse
___ leave my position
___ baptize your pet
___ fix your kid
___ write a recommendation
___ listen to you complain
___ lead the staff devotional
___ the movie
___ church
___ a date
___ sing in the choir
___ sing a solo
___ the birthday party
___ the anniversary party
___ donate
___ dance
___ chaperone
___ work for you
___ the benefit for _____
___ Bible study
___ be your youth pastor
___ be your pastor
___ usher
___ organize the Women's Ministry
___ write an article for the bulletin

As it turns out, I already have plans to...

___ be on vacation
___ lead a youth activity
___ wash my hair
___ lose my hair
___ grow old by myself
___ sleep
___ play video games
___ go out
___ skydive
___ eat
___ love Jesus in another way
___ hang myself from my ankles
___ go hunting and kill some animals
___ ignore poverty and starving children
___ give to the needs of others
___ have "me time"

____ spend time away from you
____ wax my back
____ pull my fingernails out one at a time with pliers
____ sing
____ party
____ see that movie with someone else
____ be disciplined by the church
____ work out my personal demons *(Get out!!!)*
____ lose my voice
____ be injured
____ walk across the country

I'd rather...

____ take a rain-check
____ not do it
____ die like a disciple
____ keep my issues to myself, thanks
____ you keep your issues to yourself
____ eat a rhino
____ see a New Kids on the Block reunion concert

Maybe...

____ another time?
____ next time?
____ later that day?
____ you'll stop asking me?
____ never?
____ I'll die before then?
____ hell will freeze over?
____ Jesus will come back?
____ the church will discipline me?

Salutation

____ Thanks anyway,
____ Sincerely,
____ Go to blazes,
____ Hoping you'll stop talking to me,
____ Godspeed,
____ Your friend,
____ Your enemy,
____ Your youth pastor,
____ Your pastor,
____ Yours truly,

_____

(Sign your name here)

PENTECOSTAL STAFF MEETING

BINGO

B	I	N	G	O
Manifest	Private jet	Word of knowledge	Holiness	Armani
un-	Offering	Sister	Felt	Seed
Revelation	Prophecy	**FREE** Anointing	The world	Pluralism
Fire	Hell	The Devil	Spirit-filled	Charisma
Broadcast	Tour	Power	Apostolic	Revival

BAPTIST STAFF MEETING

BINGO

Sin	Saved	Steeple	Disney	Worldly
Purpose-driven	Family life center	Hell	Brother	Mention of church down the street
Liberal	Sinner	**FREE** Baptist (no one talks about themselves as much)	Building program	Sunday school
Homo-sexual	Sin	Faith and message	Missionaries speaking in tongues	Hell
Potluck	Convention	Liberty	The Word of God	America

PROGRESSIVE CHURCH STAFF MEETING

BINGO

Contemporary	Culture	Life stage	Perception	World-class
State-of-the-art	Vision	Initiative	Equip	Video venue
Live feed on the T1 line	Lumens	**FREE** Leader	.tv	Catalyst
Lighting director	Inspire	Viral	J-Crew	Set (in reference to the music)
Set (in reference to the stage background)	Design	Campus	Values	WWASD? What would Andy Stanley do?

EMERGING CHURCH STAFF MEETING

BINGO

Village	Ecclesi-ology	Blog	Conver-sation	System
Organic	Cohort	Hemp	Friend	Volf
Liturgy	Coffee	**FREE** Community	Rhythm	Whole
Dialogue	Vibe	Kingdom of God	Environ-ment	Wright
Podcast	Missional	Ethos	Home	Creed

MAINLINE CHURCH STAFF MEETING

B	I	N	G	O
Service	Committee	Trustee	Endowment	Funeral
Organist	Rite	Justice	Robe	Choir
Memorial carpet	Building	**FREE** Calendar	Stained (glass or carpet)	Potluck
Discipline	Tradition	Picnic	Hospital visitation	Membership
Chapel	Coordinator	Education	Alarm	Altar

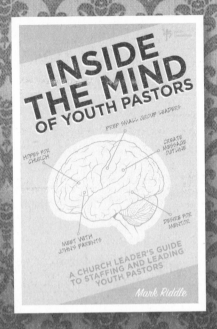

In this practical book for church leaders, you'll discover how to develop a healthy and sustainable student ministry that includes encouraging your youth pastor, engaging teens, and involving parents. Whether you already have a youth pastor or are just beginning your search, this book will help you set up your student ministry and youth pastor for health and longevity.

Inside the MInd of Youth Pastors
A Church Leader's Guide to Staffing and Leading Youth Pastors

Mark Riddle
Retail $16.99
978-0-310-28365-2

Visit www.youthspecialties.com
or your local bookstore.

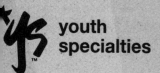

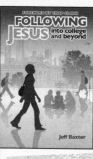

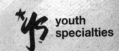